Metamorphosis

Poems of transition by
Christine Rigden

LLE NODDFA BOOKS
Warwickshire

Many of these poems have been written
for friends going through difficulties,
rather than from my personal experience.

I am thankful to them for sharing
their journeys with me.

First published in 2016 by Lle Noddfa Books,
Warwickshire, UK

christine@rigdenage.co.uk,
www.rigdenage.co.uk/christine

ISBN 978-0-9513221-3-0

Printed and bound by Lulu.com

Contents

Metamorphosis 5

Who am I 7

Still waters...8

Compass 9

Sandlings...10

Call on Him 11

Grace on water 12

Overthinking 13

Old friends 14

Hanley...15

Transition...16

Silence 17

Seasons...18

An end to summer.....................................19

Finally 20

Maelstrom..21

Journal 22

Dénouement...23

Questions...24

Gone Aground 25

Uncle Caddy's farm 26

After darkness 27

After drought..28

Resonance 29

Friendship quilt...30

Another dawn 31

Tangible solitude...32

Departure 33

Felixstowe 1953...34

Waiting..35

Winter boating 36

A winter's day..37

Forsaken..38

Recession...39

Reunion 40

Tapestry 41

So be it...42

Blessed...43

Options...44

Metamorphosis

You think
you already know me,
already have the measure of my soul.

Not so.

Experience
has changed its shape
beyond the limits of your knowledge.

Beyond
your interest, too?

Who am I

Feigning confidence, I hide
behind illusions of openness –
always reaching and seeking
from a reserved arm's length.

Though contained, I want to dance
barefoot across a polished floor
giddy with laughter and dreams.

Fragmented and intensely whole –
content and wise and desolate –
too much trouble to notice or know.

Still waters

Feelings
skim across the silence
of your face,
fleeting dragonflies
mirrored
on the still pond.

Compass

Thank you
for being the firm centre
of my world.
I may dash here and there
to listen,
hug and comfort,
write or pray –
But always circle back again
to home, and you.

Your love grounds me
in stability –
roots to my giving,
an anchor in storms.
Where would I be
without you?
Endlessly adrift
without horizons.

Thank you
for freeing me to reach out
(it's who I am
why I'm here).
But like a compass draws a circle,
I need you at my centre
to find purpose,
to be whole.

Sandlings

I am like open heath – a wildness
shaped by sun
and rain that drives or drifts;
by summer bees
that gather from rough heather;
by cautious deer and careful fires.
Shaped by woodmen
slashing gorse and birch,
evicting oak trees planted by magpies.

Without such shaping I am lost –
strangled, overwhelmed,
no longer me.
Cleansing fire brings life,
and axe makes space for growth –
for cryptic Nightjars
and Silver-studded Blues.

Call on Him

I love the Lord who heard my voice –
He heard my cry for mercy.
Because He turned His ear to me
I will call on Him forever.

Entrapped by care and felled by pain
and overcome by sorrow
I called on Him – *"Lord, save me!"*
I will call on Him forever.

> *Now be at rest again my soul*
> *for the Lord is good to you.*

I love the gracious Lord Who saves,
compassion in His eyes.
Because He guards the true in heart
I will call on Him forever.

For You, Lord, have delivered me
from stumbling and tears.
I'll walk with You now, all my days
and call on You forever.

> *Now be at rest again my soul*
> *for the Lord is good to you.*

After Psalm 116:1-9

Grace on water

Sun glints on portholes, blue winks
beyond a dance of passing shadows.
The steady thrum threads its blurred notes
through steel and wood, and bone.
Curling past her length of hull,
hushed harmonics rush and fizz.
Each moment bubbles from the last –
emerges timeless, unchanged.

Overthinking

Imagination baits me –
mother to relentless thoughts,
a fierce dance in my head
to bruise my weary mind

and snake through empty hours.
They move through the night,
trip me up in the darkness
with quiet, persistent words

loud as a headline.
They howl, and silently
bear my heart away,
worry it like a trapped mouse

stretched on the rack
of elusive sleep. Again.
My calm is worn to powder,
my resilience to zero.

This does me no service. At
night's end and dawn's threshold,
I study the lie of the land,
the yawn of distance to sanity.

Finding my balance
I take careful aim,
and stretch to jump the chasm
across into the light again.

Old friends

Do you remember the mountains that day?
We stopped by the side of a winding road
for a picnic, high over the valley.
The scattered clouds blew overhead,

their shadows dim futures above the far fields,
and grassy slopes were warmed by the sun.
We climbed the path by the careless stream,
and watched it curl through emerald folds,

swirl in pools round scattered stones.
We sat to get our breath and watched
the shadows drift. Talk flowed and lulled;
eyes met in the silence of distant dreams.

Such jewelled days glow still, from the shadows;
a friendship still sunshine across dappled years.

Hanley

The pot banks along the canal
are silent;
their broken backs
are brick
patched with concrete.
Remnants of windows
hazed with dust
almost obscure
stacks of unglazed plates
on cluttered sills
and pale drifts of unfinished pots
sit like ghosts
in the yard.

'Pot bank' is a Stoke-on-Trent expression for a pottery factory

Transition

Black branches scratch an icy sky
as cursory gold subsides.
Deep shadows cloak the listless water,
sparrows haste to hidden roosts.
The day is cut off in its prime!
Though often seen, this evening sky
so soon – just feels abrupt, misplaced.
I delay to draw the curtains,
light the fire against the cold –
pointlessly resist relentless night.

Silence

We talk and stroll
among the trees and brambles.
I make space
with a cautious question
an offer to listen.
You respond, then step aside
onto safer ground.
You say little,
listening to my chatter
seldom of any consequence –
I don't know how to interpret
your quiet.
Unvoiced questions, like rain are
falling in the silence,
turned aside by circumstance
or choice:

> *How brief was 'numb'*
> *or wide is 'empty'?*
> *How bottomless is 'dreadful'?*
> *Is time of any use at all?*

Here is silence, like a door
to close against the rain.
Yet it stands ajar, itself a question
listening to the rain
dance among the trees.

Seasons

Life has its seasons.
Friendships ebb and flow.
Close ties can be stretched
to breaking
by busyness, distance, time.

All the masks we wear
to survive our lives
keep others at arm's length –
build inner walls in layers
by years.

Time moves on,
leaves gaps in its pattern
where friends should be.
Wounds of the heart, hidden
but not healed.

An end to summer

As the autumn day awakes,
she wraps her son
in the soft routines of morning,
and time is still.

The phone shrills on the wall –
his voice fragments –
>   *"darling ... a hijack... I love you..."*
--- connections break.

She stares down at the phone,
at the clock
at weekend coats, his slippers,
the breakfast things...

and the future gapes at her feet.

Finally

The weeks will shorten
when I cease
to long for Friday
and the vacant afternoon
will taunt me
with its frequence.
However much I rail,
finality encroaches
unchanged.

I do not welcome
that day.

Maelstrom

Lord
I don't know how to handle this.

The whorls of circumstance
now turn, entwine, spin tight –
spiral down to the unknown
deep into dismay.

How do I reach You
in these darkened days?
Questions veer and multiply –
where do I begin?

I look down into the endless depth
from a high stretched wire
and close my eyes.
The maelstrom deepens beneath me

as the slow days erode.
I have only
my trust in You
for balance.

Journal

From a Vineyard shop of long ago,
this cover (soft with amber leather)
holds pages worn in edge and ink.

> *"... last night beneath the Milky Way*
> *we swam in the lagoon.*
> *Water slid like silk against my skin,*
> *phosphorescence swirled about..."*

Each day was huge – aglow or gloom:
strident dark and crashing seas
splintered the glory of the sun;
we danced on windswept slopes
hiding razor crags of loneliness.

New entries scarce as decades pass
page on empty page stares back,
watching the smooth days slip by –

> *"... called Mom tonight, and*
> *heard about her flowers..."*

Not bright, not black. A sheltered sea
lies flat beneath the same old,
same old sunset; sand and seaweed
edge the rise and fall of lifescapes
crowded with experience worn thin.

Dénouement

Long shadows
from the probing moon
stretch across the kitchen floor.

In the silent house,
an abandoned meal
lies on the table.
The phone stays mute.

A snowfield presses against
the still, black edge of forest.
The silence spreads
beyond the horizon –

wider
deeper
than she can reach.

Questions

Questions arise in heart and mind
like waves from a cold unknown.
They crash on our uncertain shores
then draw back
from the washed sands of now –
and crash again.

Questions sparkle in the sunshine,
hold awesome power in storms.
They whisper in the background
among deckchairs
and murmur across distance
and darkness.

Such tumult of the line between
our small known present
and all else
demands respect, stirs fear.
But where would life sparkle
without the splendour
of the waves?

Gone Aground

I miss the changing view outside my window
with each dawn revealing a new place
the slow blossoming of days that felt like two.

As I travelled I had bed and galley with me,
saw friends each place I went, other boaters
to greet, and easy chats by the lock side.

Gone is the need to fetch water, mend ropes.
No more cold toes on winter mornings but
I loved that hidden world, my boat was my Home.

Four walls and heating desiccate my spirit –
I miss the fire that catches when ice is outside
and the blazing welcome of my little stove.

No more intimate dinners in my snug saloon,
cosy nights in winter, towpath drinks in summer,
the security of roaming and always being home,

There's no mist rising off the dark water
outside my kitchen windows in early morning,
no deck for sitting out in dappled moonlight.

No cows, no coots, no movement;
I miss being rocked to sleep.

Oh how I miss being rocked to sleep.

Uncle Caddy's farm

July had bleached the sky again,
grimed our feet with summer dust,
serenaded us with crickets.

We swung in the apple-scented shade,
rough ropes chafed our hands,
lush grass refreshed our skin
beneath the dappled green.

Our cousin called: *Come see!*
We ran to the cool, dim barn to find
a nest of new born kittens
tumbling in the hay,
each the size of my two hands.

Later, the lumbering cows
came swaying through the open gate
ready to milk,
and swallows laced the evening air.

After darkness

"We plumb the depths within the night
yet trust", the saints of old might say -
"For after darkness comes the Light."

Some nights are grey, and sorrow slight
in terms of pain. One need not stay
to plumb the depths within the night.

Incessant battles drain the fight –
trust may let go and ebb away...
But after darkness comes the light.

Then as the anguished shadows bite,
they drown the heart in dark dismay –
and plunge to depths within the night.

When life is bathed in blackness, fright
subsumes the sense, devours the day –
"But after darkness comes the light."

The sun returns; the world, put right.
Darkness wanes. Trust shows the way
to plumb the depths within the night,
for after darkness comes the Light.

After drought

Soft mist rises
softening rain drifts
falls, silently dances
on dry ground,
seeps into baked earth.

Old, cold abandoned roots
rediscover strength
of green shoots,
yearning growth
restoring lost joy.

Resonance

She hardly ever thinks of you
these days...

Except in early spring
when a blackbird's singing
sounds the same
as when the loss was new.

Or when light glints
across a wooden floor
polished cool under naked feet.

Or when passing through the station
on the train;
or hurrying past the willow trees
en route to work.

Soundless echoes resonate
and then are still.

Friendship quilt

Together we share patchwork lives,
a collage of diverse hours –
woven textures, lines and shapes,
hued embroidery –
changing seasons in tactile guise.

Your friendship glows within my life
as spun gold thread:
First woven lavishly through a dull weft
of wearisome days
in some difficult years.

Then brief highlights scattered randomly
within life's restless texture –
here and there, now and then –
luminous and clear.

Your shining stitches appliqué
precious hours of special grace
and adorn the fleeting years
with gleaming warmth
and blessing.

Another dawn

Another dawn
steals across an empty shore –
pale refuge from the inner ring
of cockcrow.

Your tender voice entreats me,
leads me from divided self
to meet Your eyes
anew.

Today – beyond denials –
You still seek affirmation
of my sparse
and fractured love.

I come –
my brokenness made whole
in You.

Tangible solitude

Downy flakes drift and swirl
magical against the night –
softening all sounds and senses,
frosting gorse and ground.
The old familiar barren wood
now a different world –
bathed in softly glittering light,
igniting quiet exhilaration
in the tangible solitude.

Departure

A door ajar –
and sunlight filtered
through the dust
of a long-forgotten room.
Fresh laughter
laced the stillness,
discoveries
dissolved the years.
A neglected corner
was sought out
and brought alive.

Time
now secures the door again.
The light withdraws
leaving traces of warmth,
an echo of tears.

Felixstowe 1953

Wind strengthens our back as beneath
brusque darkness we push on, to join
the prior tide – still high – that awaits us
mute and now enlarged, compounded.

We search for all weakness in levees, walls,
thrust onto sluggish streets and lanes, pour
restless around houses, inexorably creep
under doors, up stairs, into sleeping rooms.

Still we grow stronger. The thunder of us
splinters darkness, ransacks all before and
weaves cries together to heighten the clamour.

Remote stars in the blackness watch us
pull fishing boats from moorings and cattle
from their fields, swipe lamps off tables, children
from their beds, drag houses from their roots.

At last the night turns, and the tide; and
we gather our strength to push on.

In January 1953 there was a particularly high spring tide, and also
especially strong north winds. A Felixstowe fisherman noted that
night that the previous high tide had not gone out. There were
devastating floods both sides of the North Sea and a total lack of
warning – while the first victims in Scotland and Lincolnshire were
drowning, the people of Suffolk were still enjoying a normal
Saturday evening.

Waiting

The moon glows low,
old ivory hanging in the trees,
shining down the river
in a crisp
and cobalt evening.

Clouds loom on the horizon
as our passive words
circle round and round
what may be.

We turn each stone again,
rake old leaves –
foraging for options,
contriving prudent actions
when all that can be done
is wait.

Winter boating

We slid through still water
in the motionless dawn.
A mantle of snow
masked the wooded margins
and even the ever-present heron
hid from the bleak sky.

A winter's day

Day dawned beneath a frigid sky
in what counts for normal now.

My friend stops for coffee
stays to lunch.

I call to my daughter to buy bread –
she comes for some change,
and goes.

We talk of scarcity and recipes
not minding the clock,
sirens an accustomed
distant background.

A rap at the door
and we notice the time.
        'That's odd – that she should knock.'

Forsaken

The chill shadow begins
on the outside -
friendless as an echo,
solitary and ignored.

The darkness widens,
creeps further in -
begins to feel deliberate,
malign.
A sense of: now deserted,
abandoned and disowned.

Then inexorably falls
the night without dawn,
the cold without warm -
now hopeless, worthless,
destitute,
alone.

> *"My God, my God -
> why have You forsaken me?"*

Recession

As the long, lavish day expires,
a streetlamp stammers
against encroaching gloom.
The chill wind
slices through all confidence,
drives the day's news along an empty street
into shadows thronged by phantoms.
A concrete wall, graffitied with fear
obstructs the feeble light
intensifies the dark.
For these uneasy hours
sanity is eclipsed, optimism blinded
in the baneful threat of night.

Reunion

I often wondered if we'd meet again,
how it would be –
if we could find words
to span the silent years.
You seemed clenched, brittle within
that familiar, careful nonchalance –
now less careful, more weary.
We sat with our drinks
as the silences came and went,
and the walls of resigned politeness
began to shift and thin.
Through chinks in your caution
I caught glimpses of the deep despair
that holds you hostage.
Words drifted, slight answers
crept through unspoken questions:
I was glad to hear past joys
amid the grasping darkness.
You were blunt --
        "No cure but miracles, or death."
Your words are heavy in my hands,
as I pray for the miracle.

Tapestry

My tapestry He weaves.
Each hue is chosen
juxtaposed in textured span
and some contrast the grey.

Thank you for being
the spun gold sunshine
and blue skies in His weaving,
wild silk in the texture of days.

So be it

My wise years
are humbled
by your simple obedience.

All choices now hold pain.
This one
leaves a cleaner wound,
no ragged guilt
to poison.

See –
my eyes are dry.
I still can smile.

Yet there's a trickle in my heart
like the slow path of rain
down a window
or a face.

Blessed

Blessed are the merciful... (Matt 5 v7)

Show compassion that wings joy
for you are the salt of the earth.
But if the salt no longer has flavour,
where will the world find mercy?

You are the light of the world –
let your actions be radiant,
deeds that glorify God and reject
the darkness of the self-righteous.

Give up revenge: losing eyes, teeth
and money to lawyers. Share restraint,
cash, clothes, miles with all who ask.
Reconcile your brother, love your foe.

Become the gift you bring to the altar.

Options

I stand still at the edge
of possibilities.
Options lap at my feet,
drag the
moments like sand from
under my toes
and heels, unsettling me
miring me
in hesitation. Too many choices
foam and
swirl about me. Gulls jeer,
time ebbs.
I still stand, feet buried in
grains of time.
I must choose, must move before
the tide comes in.

www.ingramcontent.com/pod-product-compliance
Lightning Source LLC
Chambersburg PA
CBHW060949050426
42337CB00052B/3295